Ira Singh's first novel, *The Surveyor*, was published in 2014. She teaches English Literature at Delhi University's Miranda House.

BY THE SAME AUTHOR

The Surveyor

Pilgrimage

- A Novel -

IRA SINGH

SPEAKING TIGER PUBLISHING PVT. LTD
4381/4, Ansari Road, Daryaganj
New Delhi 110002

Copyright © Ira Singh 2018

ISBN: 978-93-88070-32-4
eISBN: 978-93-88070-03-4

10 9 8 7 6 5 4 3 2 1

The moral rights of the author have been asserted.

Typeset in Bembo Std. by SŪRYA, New Delhi
Printed at ...

All rights reserved.
No part of this publication may be reproduced, transmitted,
or stored in a retrieval system, in any form or by any
means, electronic, mechanical, photocopying,
recording or otherwise, without the
prior permission of the publisher.

This book is sold subject to the condition that it shall not,
by way of trade or otherwise, be lent, resold,
hired out, or otherwise circulated, without
the publisher's prior consent, in any form
of binding or cover other than that in
which it is published.

For
Jamal

If I were called in/To construct a religion/I should make use of water./And I should raise in the east/A glass of water/Where any-angled light/Would congregate endlessly.

—Philip Larkin, 'Water'

Yet the illusion of meaning recurred, much as you tried to resist it; like childhood, I said, which we treat as an explanatory text rather than merely as a formative experience of powerlessness.

—Rachel Cusk, *Transit*

Pilgrimage

She sees her father strapped down on a gurney, face covered by the mask of a portable ventilator, blood blooming along the path of the hastily inserted tube in his wrist, life beating erratic, quick, at his neck; the nurse, muttering into his cell phone, jiggling the stand to which the drip is connected; she hears the slosh-slosh of urine in the plastic bag on the side of the gurney, hears her mother's prayers.

Her cell phone rings. It is Vicky, her brother, in a panic; he will take the first flight he can get, he says. She talks calmly about the situation, she reassures him.

Her phone rings again; a relative, bemoaning the fact that her brother isn't here to do his duty.

The driver stops for a pee, apologetically. She emerges, too, from the back of the hard-benched brutal interior of the vehicle for a minute, looking anxiously over her shoulder, cell phone to her ear. The air hits her face, moist and smelling richly of cow dung. Dogs, yammering, slink into the shadows. The relative talks on. She is exhorted to be calm, philosophical and wise, to believe in the power of the Almighty.

Devotees roar past. They are called kanwariyas. In this season, the season of rain, in a month named after the rain, they walk down highways with gaudy tinsel-covered pots of holy water strapped across their shoulders. They are worshippers of Shiva and must, at the end of their arduous journey, empty these laden pots at their village temples, please the god with their fervour.

They have been seen for years on this route; stork-like they'd made their way, flash of bony legs and rain pouring down upon them they balanced their loads and walked on.

Now they race past, waving saffron flags.

PILGRIMAGE

She sees, in quick succession, men on a pair of motorbikes with no silencers, yelling, a tempo with flashing lights atop and then a decorated truck, two glittering mini temples inside and devotees trudging alongside, streamers floating behind, a diesel genset packed into its roomy interior and a disco beat thumping, its volume ratcheted up.

She gets into the ambulance, the air-conditioning envelops her, neon within. It is considered state of the art: shiny, stocked with gleaming gadgets, expensive to hire, the first of its kind in the small town they have come from. This desperate journey to the city was the result of a doctor's pronouncement in an ill-equipped hospital; he said he needed his sole working ventilator for a burn victim, a young man whose wife, two small children and dazed old parents were huddled outside, sobbing. The implication was obvious, her father was not needed in this world the way the young man was, bandages on his bare muscular chest, eyes taped shut.

Frightened, they had decided swiftly then to take her father away, decided under pitiless tube lights outside the rudimentary ICU, odours of illness and inability [bloodied dressings, bed pans] mingling with antiseptic and phenyl in the corridor. Her mother rushed home and came back clutching a small bag containing her husband's night clothes, his shaving things, two hand towels and some Dettol handwash; she grabbed his bulky medical file from the staff and climbed into the ambulance with her little clutch of velvet-bound holy books tied with string.

Her father stirs, she wants to tell him they'd got the ambulance at a discount, the owner knew him. Instead she is forced to look away from the punishment of him stretched out on the rack. Her mother is of no use to her, she has not moved, she sits cross-legged on the floor next to the gurney, head covered, and mutters. Trucks and tempos pass them, they overtake yet others, the driver swift with the wailer, violent explosions of noise that push against the sealed windows. Her father cannot hear these. Her mother, she thinks, chooses not to.

Increasingly the landscape of these great dusty highways is dominated by saffron, the colour of a faith. On the broken-down walls at the edges of fields fringed by ragged rows of eucalyptus, there have always been hastily scrawled invocations, on billboards and pillars pictures of saints and the gods, holy men's discourses blaring from podiums and TVs, always those makeshift shrines with diyas flickering below peepal trees and labyrinthine processions carrying statues of decorated deities to the rivers.

All that magnified, exaggerated, distorted.

She has seen camps that seek to make kanwariyas comfortable, they are given food and drink, shelter, they are given respect; loud speakers, triumphal fervour, the piety and obeisance of people, and plastic waste, mark these camps.

She has seen those other camps, too, the camps of refugees from the tall fields of Muzaffarnagar not that long ago, tarpaulin blue and flapping and thick mud everywhere as children, uncharacteristically quiet, played, women, bewildered, wept, and young men [impotent, uncertain] talked wildly of revenge. Old men gathered and talked of compensation. They talked of citizenship.

~

These dark hours limp past, her father no worse, she thinks, no worse, though his face, lit up in passing, is twisted with knowledge and suffering.

Vicky swallowed up by marriage and suburbia in America, she had become an odd companion to her father; she went home often, the violent tussles of the years of her extended youth behind them. He had taken to writing her long emails, reporting feverishly on everything he read about, on black holes, genomics, cryonics. He was particularly excited by cryonics, its hubris. He sent her drafts of his irate letters to government functionaries, he became attached to the phrase *senior citizens*. He had started, recently, to unearth articles detailing Nehru's vision for the nation. He had a series of quotations from the scriptures to counteract invective; to her great relief she'd found that he was, quite vehemently and emphatically, *not* in agreement with the killing unfolding.

He even boasted about her regularly, about her work with victims of what he called, in an odd Americanism, terror. The phrase saved him, she had realized, from fully acknowledging the *actual* nature of her work and the particular pathology of genocide, allowed him to not completely recognize the people she helped, the people whose suffering she was witness to.

She cannot accustom herself to this moment of reckoning, her father before her unseeing, the vividness of him in life, this bloodied almost end. His hands, feeble on the thin sheet covering him, are swollen, each finger twice its size, redstone ring stuck.

He always went to bed with a torch, a bottle of eye drops and a little vial of homeopathic pills for some disorder or the other; they lolled, this trio, by his pillow. He worshipped locks, combination locks, spinning dials, he massaged old locks with machine oil, kept an old camel-coloured toilet bag filled with them, their companion keys neatly tagged. She remembers his fetishes, who he was, who he *is*, as they hurtle through the night.

She is crying silently, snot dripping. Many, many years ago, before Vicky was born, he made a butterfly net for her, then he taught her to let the butterflies escape and they streamed out of her net and into the world; he has been in her world from the beginning.

The nurse plays games, sends messages, circulates jokes. He grazes the port, adjusts the drip needlessly, fiddling. Her mother seems oblivious to this; it is she, Monica, who admonishes him, crouches by the stand, reprimands him when he talks. The smell of cooked food and dung fires when she pushes her window open briefly, just for a moment, breathing in the noxious heady warm smell of the night, a minor escape from the arctic cold of the ambulance, of the sight of her father whom, she is convinced, is shivering, though perhaps it is just the movement of the vehicle that makes her think so, she wishes they had got a blanket, she wishes she had gone home instead of her mother, she would have got biscuits too.

She is violently, ashamedly, hungry.

The nurse, surprising her, says madam, it

will not be good for him. He jerks his head in the direction of the sick man, her father. She pushes the window back in place obediently. She cannot anymore look upon the sight before her, she asks the driver to stop for a minute and moves to the front seat where a drop of water, with unceasing regularity, falls on her right foot from the air-conditioning vent above.

They are stuck at a railway crossing; two men skewered in the glare of the headlights, loping across, a boy selling roasted corn at this time of night, familiar filth and stench, urine smell powerful even within.

Beside them is a tempo traveller filled with pilgrims frantic in the perennial season of pilgrimages, they come from cities they have been promised will turn *smart*, cities full of sewage; it has been decreed that they will bathe themselves in the sacred river.

Everywhere the night is frightening, no

country for arguments now, trucks and tempos whizzing past to their destinations, drivers worried about their cargo of restive animals, dead animals, skins and bones, hide, the makings of leather; drivers worried about their names and about their prayer-caps, about the malevolence and speed of rumours, about the cold fact-checking of the mob.

Here the road broad and tree trunks washed with lime stand out in the damp air. Here the highway.

~

The driver suggests they take a detour to avoid the kanwariyas and they speed and screech down relatively quiet roads in the deep night, hamlets deserted, a few scrawny dogs sleeping fitfully outside little huts.

This is sugarcane country; bullock carts and tractors laden with it lumber across these districts. The fumes of sugar manufacturing are everywhere.

PILGRIMAGE

She had never thought of the town, the swathe of land where she grew up as part of *Western UP*, a category, a classification. Now that is inescapable, it is counted in terms of the religion calculus and its demographic mined, analysed, colour coded, its capacity for hatred, for murder, exemplified, distilled, in the photograph of Akhlaq on TV screens, that unbearably poignant passport-sized photograph with a red background.

She sees this intimately familiar countryside differently now; she sees the odd, perhaps illusory, innocence of temples and mosques, cheek by jowl, marred.

They come, suddenly, to a halt. The road ahead is blocked. The driver turns on his wailer. The dense stretch turns out to be a collection of vehicles inching along, packed with kanwariyas dancing to loud disco bhajans. Some run behind each truck, carrying batons and bottles of water, daak kanwariyas, postmen. They are unmoved by the high-pitched yowling of the ambulance, this tone that signifies impending doom. Its noise is drowned out by theirs [deafening, unapologetic].

Young men, half naked, dance. They wear baggy shorts, track pants, orange lungis. Their T-shirts proclaim Bum Bhole and Bhole Nath, in praise of the god, they wave the tricolour and shout Bharat Maata ki Jai, in praise of the motherland. Saffron banners flutter in the meagre night air. Each banner speaks of origins, of the village, the place from which these particular young men have journeyed, how far they have come on their quest.

The driver turns to her, he pushes open the connecting window, the nurse shaken out of his WhatsApp-induced stupor. Her mother comes out of the trance of prayer. The driver calls her mataji.

We can't move them, the driver says to all of them worriedly. They don't like interference.

PILGRIMAGE

Their shivir has been set up nearby, that's why they are moving so slowly now.

He means their camp, where they will have their feet massaged by willing volunteers, where they will be assured by the minions of the state that they are protected admired revered.

He says a riot is possible if they are moved. The word danga, riot, fills her with alarm.

She watches the appalling spectacle, momentarily outside the increasing urgency of the situation.

The driver says tenderly, watching them dance, [hockey sticks in their hands] poor things. Many die on this pilgrimage every year. They are killed by speeding trucks and cars, by Mohammedans too, deliberately.

She interrupts him rudely, snapping back into the moment. She cannot listen to this.

You need to move them, she says.

They are doing the work of God, he continues to muse, why blame them, how is it their fault, they go to get that sacred water and they walk barefoot, on stones and through the dust of highways, through fields, they travel only in worship, to fulfil their vows. Mohammedans wire their fields and the current kills these poor boys when they pass through. That is why they have started using trucks to travel, because of these people.

My father will die, she says, now not listening to this casual, unconscious venom, not even, anymore, responding to it.

The driver is a good man, she is sure of that, he understands suffering, he will help her.

My father will die if we don't reach the hospital soon, she says again. Please do something.

The driver gets down, he goes towards the men.

She finds she is weeping again, she has uttered the word death and it has become real, she imagines her father unmoving, without breath or blood.

Their journey has ground to a halt in front of the faithful; the beat gets louder, every surface nearby rings, vibrates from the noise.

A hot thin moon rides above them.

The road is lit up by neon from their portable generator, the air thick with diesel fumes, they are *producing* electricity, consuming it, they are sufficient unto themselves, their lives till now [unremarked, unredeemed] pure in these moments of elevation.

She watches the driver reason with the leader of the young men, who has hopped off a motorbike and who wears an orange T-shirt with a matching pair of shorts. It is obvious he wears no underwear.

He wears sneakers.

[Weren't they supposed to be barefoot? Weren't they supposed to suffer?]

The young man gesticulates angrily. The driver folds his hands. She sees before her, in gestures, a drama of supplication and appeasement.

PILGRIMAGE

Her mother says, from the back, Mona.

She gets down. She marches towards the man, who turns and stares.

It must be her cropped hair, her jeans and shirt, she thinks, she is used to the staring.

She must make him understand. The driver says to her, madam, go back, he will not listen to you. His voice is raised. Perforce.

She says in a rusty imperious voice, tears banished now, falling into a recognizable idiom, my father is critical. Let the ambulance go past.

This head gyrator, mechanically touching his lips and forehead in a superstitious gesture, implores her to speak only of good fortune, Shubh shubh bolo, he says.

She says, urgently, we have to go to the hospital.

He gestures at his comrades, in motion, ostensibly lost in worship.

I cannot do anything Aunty, he says.

He wears a sacred thread on his brawny wrist, a holy smear on his forehead.

PILGRIMAGE

He turns away.

Absurdly, she finds herself as offended by the appellation as by the gesture.

She grabs his arm. It is tattooed, inked with portraits of armed goddesses. They leap out at her, blue in the lurid glare. She has never touched a working-class man before. He shakes her hand off roughly, clearly not electrified by her touch, seeing it, evidently, as a breach of propriety.

She says, holding her phone up, I will WhatsApp your photo to the media. Everyone will know you stopped a man from reaching the hospital, you denied him treatment. Is this your religion?

The rhetoric comes unbidden to her lips.

The nurse looks impressed. He has hopped out of the ambulance. The machines are on within, hissing, rattling.

The kanwariya pauses in turning away. The word religion, it seems, signifies only authority [brazen, brassy]. The word media holds for him, though, a multitude of meanings.

The nurse proffers his opinion, that WhatsApp is sabse best, sabse. The kanwariya looks at the nurse: a man from his world, yet trained, earning a living.

The driver says, folding his hands: Bhai, I am begging you to move them. We have to reach the hospital.

They have worked as a team, they are united by this triumph as the kanwariya calls to the faithful in gestures and in mime, they cluster around him, indignant. They listen, they scatter, their vehicles move, slowly, painfully. A path opens up.

The ambulance roars to life, wailer on.

Her mother's prayers rise and fall, they rise and fall.

~

PILGRIMAGE

Smudged beginnings of dawn when they pull up outside the city hospital, a grey stucco-fronted affair. She hears the driver's muttered incantation as the nurse pulls the gurney down.

It is wheeled swiftly, her mother and she on each side, into the building.

Transgressions

When I met Ajay and his family I was twenty-four, living in a working-women's hostel, red brick and respectable, the stench of stale food down the corridors, three to a room and filthy bathrooms, everything you feared about being an adult, and a *working woman* at that. The saving grace, though, were the surroundings. In those years before the big multiplex with its attendant cafes and bars and fast-food hangouts came up, this was a quiet residential colony with canopies of gigantic trees and a sense of comfort. I often went for long walks down those tree-lined roads, stopping, on the way back, at a sweetshop which sold chaat and samosas and fresh mithai.

It reminded me of home.

I did not cultivate any acquaintance in the

hostel. I was a snob, really, and prided myself on my passion for psychology, in which I had begun research. I worked as an assistant with a lecturer from college and I already found my job routine, but I needed it because my parents no longer sent me money. Our last meeting had not ended well, I was *not* going to get married, I was not going to *settle down*, I said, I was going to study.

I packed my bags and left in a rage. They sent my brother Vicky racing after me to Delhi. I refused to listen to his hectoring.

I was, I think, almost used to the pattern of my life, fixed and resolute, when everything I will recount here began.

I met them on a blustery day in the middle of January. The hostel was particularly dark and gloomy that day. It was a Saturday, and all the clerks and stenographers I lived with had the day off from their government jobs and were occupying themselves usefully by oiling their hair and listening to the radio. The television was on in the common room, a game of cricket was being devoured, but I was preparing for a party.

The de-addiction centre where I volunteered twice a month had put me in touch with a family which had once been in rehab. I had called them, marvelling at the idea of an entire family out of rehab, already anticipating the research I would do to prepare for my thesis, a study of family dynamics and substance abuse. They were extremely friendly on the phone, at least the woman I spoke to was. She asked me to a party on Saturday, that'll be a nice way of getting to know us, she added. I took her address and asked for directions and thanked her very politely and, accordingly, I was going to a party that raw Saturday night in January, so I had to wash my hair—luckily, it was short—with ice-cold water in the presence of three well-fed rats that peered inquisitively out at me from the drain, but I didn't mind. I borrowed an iron from one of my roommates and ironed a pair of black corduroys and took out a suede jacket that Shireen, my closest friend from college, had sent me from the States.

The house I directed the auto-rickshaw to was an old yellow building, squat, slightly faded, as though it had been exposed to the elements too long. I liked this neighbourhood, its casual air, the main market with its brave old shops, and on that cold night this house seemed the most wonderful place, porch light on, potted plants lining the driveway. When I came to the front door—which, like all South Delhi houses, was actually a side door—I saw a little row of bells. I pressed the first one and, after a minute, the door was opened by a sullen boy with shifty eyes, who directed me to the first floor.

I found myself in a high-ceilinged room illuminated by a standing lamp and by light from the street, orange and lush, pouring in through the windows. But it was the sound that made the room alive, six powerful speakers and a group I learnt later was called, simply, The Band. The music was deliciously loud, and there was a sense of suppressed excitement in the air, as though anything could happen, the sign of a good party. There were maybe fifteen people in the room, a few more on the strip of balcony, and a woman came up to me as I entered and said artlessly, I'm Asma, and you must be Monica. I wasn't sure you'd be able to get to know us at a party, but at least we could meet and chat a bit. You could always interview us later.

She spoke a little breathlessly, and her voice was soft, difficult to hear above the drumming in the background. I examined her with the greatest interest as she spoke, not deaf to the nuances of the 'us' she spoke of so freely. Asma had a face that should have been framed, and it was, in fact, by swathes of curls. I saw a pair of finely arched eyebrows and thick lashes, and a mole, suggestive near her wide mouth, the lips a purple pink, the marks of cigarettes stamped upon them. She was smoking then, too, I remember, and she said, come and be introduced. So I met several people very quickly, as happens at parties, and I was given the glass of Campa Cola I requested and I stood in a corner for a moment, contemplating my surroundings.

The room had several paintings, the curtains were green silk and somewhat grand, in contrast to the sofas, which were several and faded brown, though I noticed that someone had made a bit of an effort and thrown colourful shawls over two of them. They were pushed to the walls, as was a rocking chair with a Tibetan prayer rug on it. There was a sitar in a corner and, cut into the slightly flaking walls, built-in shelves that contained stacks of cassettes.

I had absorbed some of this, trying not to look out of place, when Asma came back and stood by me. She passed me a joint, which I accepted. I liked hash, I liked the ironic distance it gave me and the way it stimulated the imagination and sex. I never drank, though, after many dreadful experiences I was not enamoured of the wobbly, foolish, melancholic state it got me into.

By now people were dancing, and Asma was asking where do you stay, Monica?

I told her about the working-women's hostel and quickly embellished my recent rat experience for her, though it didn't require embellishing, it was all perfectly true. I had always been good at telling funny stories, and I made the rats the principal characters till she laughed a great deal and her perfect face melted into teeth and frizzy hair in the dimly lit room. There was a momentary hiatus in the sound level in the room and a voice asked, what are you laughing at, Di?

Meet Monica, she's going to work on

us. We'd better be careful, Asma added, still laughing.

Nice to meet you, Monica, I'm Ajay, he said, holding out a large hand. He held a joint in his other, and I was suddenly slightly shocked by the two of them and their familiar relationship with hash—weren't they supposed to be out of rehab?

Nice to meet you, too, I said, or something equally banal, and then the music started again—Led Zeppelin's 'All My Love'.

Is the rest of the family here, too, I asked politely, above the melancholy seduction of the song. Asma and Ajay turned to each other and said, simultaneously, of course. Then they laughed, and Ajay said charmingly, don't worry, you can work on all of us soon.

His spectacles glinted in the light. He was tall, much taller than me, his face firm-jawed, intelligent.

We spent the next hour talking, talking, in

thrall to each other, ignoring everybody, and when the party was beginning to thin, Ajay, holding my gaze deliberately, slipped in a tape.

Robbie Robertson, he said, already educating me about music. You've heard this?

No, I said, blushing a little.

It sounded like the singer was *reciting* a sex act to a weird, deliberate rhythm.

Should we dance, Ajay asked. I assented, and we danced, solemnly, like it was a rite of passage, to that shockingly sexual song, to *catch the blue train / to places never seen before / look for me / somewhere down the crazy river.* And the chorus, *somewhere down the crazy river.*

That Saturday night ended, for me, at two in the morning outside the gate of the hostel. They insisted on waking the bewildered white-stubbled guard up and telling him they were my relatives and he had to take care of me and make sure I reached my room safely, which he did, looking avuncular all the while. The air was very cold, and the smell of hash was in my hair and on my clothes and it seemed to me I had travelled a great distance from the person I had been when I ironed my corduroys several hours earlier.

I had travelled the city all right, a slight fog beginning to bank against the car windows, diesel and exhaust scent in the cold night air. We had been to the streets next to Lal Quila, its red sandstone lit in the night, to buy dope from shady pushers who never slept, unlike their vagrant customers who slept the sleep of purchased oblivion under dirt-encrusted blankets. In the car we sang Kishore Kumar, or rather, Ajay sang—he sang like a dream, always melodious and in tune—he sang 'Yeh Shaam Mastaani' and everyone else hummed and yodelled, Asma chain-smoked and two hangers-on, Shankar and Sumit, whom I disliked from the beginning, drank rum and Thums Up from plastic bottles and Ajay made us laugh; we drove north in the sulphur lights and then back south on the Ring Road and the city looked wide, luscious, inviting.

I stumbled to bed more than slightly stoned, already obsessed, already slightly afraid of seeing him again, remembering the way he held my hand at parting, remembering how he felt against me when we danced.

I wasn't going to call, I told myself, I had no easy access to a phone in the first place. I was also busy in libraries; I hadn't even been able to go to the de-addiction centre in the last week as the professor I worked for had a hundred details for me to go through and check, she was writing a research paper for publication and also preparing to go to Chile. It was still a very big thing to go abroad in those days and we were still dazzled by unknown places; perhaps we hadn't watched the travel shows long on TV, or perhaps they had not yet been invented.

I *do* remember being very cold that winter

and I associated Chile with the sun. It was freezing in the library, I wore two sweaters and a jacket as I worked; I still remember that, even though so many details of that time now seem half-invented, as if I have wilfully constructed a set against which I play out imagined feelings.

I remember, though, the hard facts of the external world: the Bombay riots had just subsided, that bloodletting that had even the most deadened witnesses of riots stunned, it seemed any horror, though, was permissible after the fall of the masjid [images of those lichen-softened domes being hacked at by triumphant hordes waving saffron stay with me till today].

I heard from him the next day, the next afternoon, to be precise. I was still recovering from the night; distanced, as usual, from the Sunday reality of the hostel—women in housecoats with cardigans buttoned and salwars underneath, eating chana-puri at the dhaba. He called on the unreliable telephone near the warden's office. It was too soon, and at the same time it wasn't; I had wanted him to call, but I also wanted him to come see me with flowers, or declarations, or both: the desires of youth, after all, are inexplicable, but it is clear that they demand sacrifice and worship.

Come over, he said peremptorily.

I don't know.

I wanted him, at the very least, to come pick me up.

Just take an auto and come. His voice became intimate. We had a great time yesterday, didn't we? And Di was asking about you, too.

All right, I'll come in the evening.

I put the phone down and took in my surroundings like a somnambulist. I had classes tomorrow, and I had to meet my guide. Tomorrow's Monday, anyway, so I'll be too busy from then onwards to go over, I might as well go today. I can't wash my hair again, I thought, and then I thought: I have to wash my hair.

In the event, Asma called, too, but on the warden's number, and when I heard her voice I immediately felt bad I hadn't called, as I'd promised I would. Come and see us, she said plaintively, you didn't even really get a chance to talk to Ajju, forget Alok and Ritu. Come and have dinner.

I had a sense, from the beginning, that she liked me a great deal—later I would see how deeply reserved she was with most people. Dinner tonight, she said again, insistently, and I said yes, of course, because I really wanted to be back in that room with its crude grandeur.

But it's not a party. It'll be just us, okay? See you.

The warden watched me throughout as I spoke to Asma. Her living room was in shades of orange, she looked like she lived inside a very rancid fruit. I stumbled a little on the faux woollen tufted carpet as I left.

That evening the shifty eyed boy [poor thing, he wasn't older than seventeen, I now noticed] ushered me into a room downstairs, a great slab of a room almost identical to the one upstairs. As I entered, I saw a photograph, black and white and lavishly mounted; and as I was looking at it I heard Ajay behind me saying, that's my mother.

Oh, I said, turning around, a little flustered to be discovered peering at it, she's beautiful. I sounded foolish and naïve.

She was an actress.

But of course; that was why those eyes, eyeliner-defined, that self-conscious grace, had seemed familiar. If my memory served me right, she was a reasonably well-known actress, hadn't she died recently? All this flashed through my mind as I made the appropriate noises. We turned away from the photograph and Ajay started to tell me a story about his mother and a famous director and all the while we looked at each other.

January held us imprisoned in its clutches; grey, chill, obdurate.

I was beginning to feel a little awkward when Asma came flying down the stairs in what I would come to recognize as her distinctive leap. She was always in a hurry to get to a room, and when she reached she would retreat, marshal her forces, light a cigarette, frowning absently, her face momentarily crumpled.

So, how are you? Ajju, get us drinks, hurry up. Where's everyone else, go and call them.

Well, I'll have to. Got to get the drinks from upstairs, he said with a faint trace of irony as he exited.

It would be rude to ask why he should get the drinks, I thought, but Asma—that queer mix of frankness and utter, impenetrable reserve—said, Ajju doesn't work much, you know, we support him, Alok and I, that is. Sometimes he gets a job for a while but he's still looking around for what suits him. He's really interested in theatre, you know. She launched into a long summary of his acting career in school.

I asked, in the pause that followed her account, how old is he?

He's twenty-nine, she said, not taking offence. Deliberately, I think, she did not want me to see him as deviant.

The room had a jumble-sale-like air, I'd noticed: it looked both incomplete and already finished, doomed to stay that way forever. A bookcase in the corner had books unevenly stacked in no particular order, I was to discover later; Freud jostled with Chandler; Bellow, Prem Chand, Dostoevsky were cheek by jowl with translations of the Upanishads and Swami Vivekananda.

Asma, noticing my gaze on the books, said, Nana was a great reader, Ajay takes after him.

You know, the ground floor is Ajay's, Ma used to stay here when she came.

We live in descending order, she added, grinning. I'm the oldest, and I have the barsati, and then there's Alok and finally Ajju. Well, there's Shawna, but she doesn't live here.

Shawna, it transpired, was the youngest.

I asked Asma about her mother, determined to start asking questions that would, perhaps, lead to a finished and bound piece of my own some day. I couldn't lose touch with the original reason for being here, I thought, however attracted I was to Ajay.

Well, said Asma, she was an actress and we didn't live with her; we lived with our grandparents, in this house, because she was in Bombay and so was our father. He was a music director; in fact, he still lives there, alone. He's very attached to the city, he's lived there all his adult life.

So you never lived with your parents, all of you together?

She gave me a sideways glance.

No, she replied, how could we? They didn't live together, she had her own place in Bombay, and she travelled a lot, in any case, while shooting.

So you sort of brought yourself up? I asked, a little uncomfortably.

No, it wasn't really like that. Nana and Nani were here.

She was interrupted by the entrance of the suspicious shifty eyed boy, and, hard on his heels, Ajay, who looked cheerful as he eyed the tray the boy carried, stacked with bottles of soda and an ice bucket, preliminaries of better things to come. Prem, he commanded, go and get the bottles from the landing, I've kept them there. Oh, and remind Sahib and Memsahib to come downstairs, we have a guest.

Ajay loved playing host, it was in his blood, Asma always said that.

They were on their second drinks when

Sahib and Memsahib came downstairs. By this time, I had gathered more details of their early upbringing: schools gone to, a grandmother who adored them, indulged them. Behind this edifice, carefully constructed, a volatile, peripatetic mother, a distant father.

Ajay and I looked at each other often; he had beautiful hands, I noticed, elegant and sinewy, though his fingertips were stained brown with nicotine. He seemed, in the main, content to let Asma talk, though he chipped in with details and told some funny stories about school; smoking hash in the loo, bunking football, hallucinating through mathematics classes.

It was agreed that Maths could, in any case, feel like hallucinations, particularly Algebra, because of its almost entirely *notional* character, said Asma.

Alok was a big bear of a man, dressed in a checked shirt and jeans and expensive leather slip-ons. He never seemed to feel the cold.

When he smiled his face creased up like Asma's, but there was no real resemblance between the three of them.

Ritu, Alok's wife, was a mass of limbs. She wore shorts, tight faded blue denim shorts, gorgeous long legs on display, a grey sweatshirt with a Hard Rock Café sign on it, flip flops. She had pink nail paint on her toenails and badly bitten fingernails, a face grey with experience, not fine-featured but wry, nose out of proportion, wide mouth; one of those women with ugly faces and great bodies who have good lay written all over them.

They were as warm as Asma and Ajay, who were, by now, consuming their whisky with fine abandon.

Don't you ever feel cold, Ritu, asked Asma.

You know I don't, you guys should face winter in Boston and then see.

But the houses are heated, objected Ajay.

I know, but this winter still seems mild.

Prem, she said loudly in her pronounced Punjabi-American accent, get some ice.

Come on Ritu, when were you last in Boston, Asma asked tetchily.

Two years ago, actually, she answered, after a brief pause. Have you forgotten?

Oh right, that's when you were in rehab.

A brief silence descended. Asma thought Ritu a spoilt brat, Ritu resented supporting Ajay and Asma was protective of him but I did not know all this then, I did not occupy the privileged position I was later to, so I merely felt on edge, unsettled by their sniping at each other. That feeling didn't last long, it was replaced with dope and mellowness and laughter. It grew very late that night and Asma rolled endless joints, her fingers sorting, threading through the marijuana leaves, separating the good from the chaff. Alok produced a powerfully fragrant stubby bit of hash which was lit and crumbled and revered and smoked.

Asma always had her tin with her, an old tin that had once contained foreign cigarettes. It looked a burnished gold in the dim light of those endless evenings or on bright Sunday mornings, when sunlight would leach through the windows and fall aslant on the shabby old furniture in those rooms, bring sly illusory hope to walls scarred with cigarette smoke.

We listened to Leonard Cohen that night because Ritu loved Cohen: *I love you in the morning/your kisses deep and warm/your head upon the pillow/like a sleepy golden storm.*

I stayed the night.

~

South Campus, Delhi University's other campus, its wild other, was a stark mix of green cover and barren land. The great red rock faces of the Aravalli leered in one direction. Construction work, that euphemism which signifies making nature hospitable to habitation, continued all day and the deafening sound of drills echoed, buildings being hewn out of rock. Turn your steps away and you would find yourself at the other end of the campus, at the canteen, a recess in the wall attached to a shabby room filled with broken-down furniture and the smell of coffee and idlis.

That's where I went on Monday morning, I had fled the house while everybody was asleep, Ajay snoring, taken an autorickshaw and then a Mudrika [we called them Mudrakers in college, those efficient buses that plied only up and down the Ring Road] to reach the campus.

I had to process the night, escape its clutches to examine where I was.

When we shut the bedroom door behind us nobody had been surprised. They bade us good night with the greatest good cheer—we could hear Ritu humming Cohen tunelessly all the way up the stairs—and in that benedictory lamp light, as we held each other for the first time, I thought myself wildly fortunate. We made love, oddly enough without much fumbling or awkwardness, familiar, as happens sometimes, and then we cuddled for hours, slipping in and out of sleep; I was stoned and he was drunk and stoned and we leaked a combined new tenderness, it's been so long, he said, so long.

I discovered his shape, and the feel of his hair and those hands on me. I woke early, though, to Ajay's snoring, to the sounds of the house and the clattering on the streets through the windows. My mouth tasted of nicotine and hash, my cheeks flushed and sore from being rubbed with stubble; I moved slowly, loath to leave, desperate to leave.

I had to ask myself, sitting in that canteen, what I was doing, what implications it had for my research, why I should be so unreasonably and instantly attracted to Ajay.

Perhaps, I thought, it was the furthest extent of my usual perversity, this seeking out of the damned. This according to Shireen, whose father had once locked her in her bedroom for a month after discovering she had a boyfriend, her mother had to climb in through the window using the maali's ladder to give her some food.

I missed Shireen more every day: we'd studied together hours, unpeeled the psyche, mimicked, *graded* our mainly brutal lovers for each other.

I heaved myself out of my chair and went to meet my guide, a dapper man with a wicked little goatee and an incisive mind, on whom I had had the most intense crush the year before when I met him at a seminar in the university.

My ability to dissemble appalled me; I was calm, coherent and certain. We discussed the shape of the thesis, its framework, the structuring of interviews. He asked me about the family—how many members, what my research would be attempting to articulate. He seemed pleased with the answers I gave him, and even more pleased by the textbook perfection of these subjects. You would, after all, have to be very lucky to find an entire family of addicts to illustrate the causes and patterns of drug abuse.

There's another sister, I believe, Shawna volunteered. She lives in Bombay, they don't have very much to do with her. The strange thing is, she hasn't ever done drugs. In fact, she disapproves thoroughly of this lot.

Is she the youngest? he asked.

Yes, the youngest. It seems very peculiar, though, that the others should be so affected by what was, by all accounts, an unconventional upbringing, while the youngest child remained entirely unaffected.

Not unaffected, perhaps, he replied thoughtfully, equally affected, but her strategy has been to distance herself from all of them. The youngest often protects herself or himself, the damage is done differently.

And distance herself from the memory of their mother, I added. She's very close to the father, Asma says, she lives near his place, takes care of him.

Asma, while she was telling me about Shawna the day before, said she didn't have a single photograph of the mother anywhere in her flat.

I suppose, he said, it's doubtful whether making memorials to her is better.

Give me a rough draft of the first chapter soon, he added. It's easy in such circumstances to think the thesis will write itself but more often than not it doesn't. He smiled wryly.

Stay focused, these sorts of subjects are notoriously slippery. And make sure you record your interviews. Transcribing an interview is an art, you are able to have the necessary distance from the subject in the interim.

Remember, he said in parting, nothing can beat the empirical.

I was in love with the family and they with me. Ajay and I played out our affair against the backdrop of these claims. I could never separate him from any of them, and our days together sometimes seemed like an extended conversation that I had been having with one of the others.

It was like being under siege, those first few months; I went to work from the house and came back there, to the lamplight and the joints.

I only went to the hostel when absolutely necessary, to pick up my things.

The warden had started looking at me as if I was dangerous.

It seemed miraculous that, the year I had needed most desperately to be adopted, I had been, and that I had been swept away to a place where I could practically cease to be myself, or where I could be the best version of myself: charming, confident, likeable, not the girl who stormed out of the house or the tormented child or the sly teenager, or all of these.

I was always telling myself, in those early days, that I was there for the research, and in a way I was. But even as I said so, and believed it, there was enough in me that didn't lie to know that I was there mainly because I was wanted; we were close all at once and it stayed that way. I remember Ajay singing, performing, the love songs of the Rolling Stones: *Angie, when will those clouds all disappear?/where will it lead us from here?* and *My sweet lady Jane/when I see you again/your servant am I/and will humbly remain.*

I remember the long pulls on the bong passed around ritually some evenings, the gurgle of the water, a dim room and a circle of people, jokes about pass the peace pipe man. Ritu made doughnuts for afters, she actually *made* them and they flew off the plates and into our mouths, oh the taste of sugar, the wanting sugar and chocolate and lemon cake, I took a course, she said. When I was wasted, she added, and everybody cracked up.

Lemon cake with lemon sauce and upside down pineapple cake and brownies, she baked and baked till all of upstairs and downstairs smelled of it. I remember a picnic Ritu organized, the city in a green and flowering February, the taste of dope in the shadows of the tombs, sunlight refracted through lattice work, and inside, in the cool, pigeons bashing against walls and *Bunty loves Sonia* etched painstakingly into marble; Asma, sloshed and silly, doing a mock cabaret to 'Monica Oh My Darling', all of us panting obligingly alongside, a cricket match in the neighbourhood park on a Sunday afternoon with crates of beer lugged up to the terrace after; The Band singing 'Who Do You Love' and Traffic's *Feelin' all right/not feelin' too good myself*, and the rush of wanting and waiting for Ajay that, combined with the dope, stretched everything high, so that when we made it to his room, the world outside with no claims on us, none, we would be so buzzed we would fuck practically in our clothes; against the door, standing up.

Then the darkness.

Thus that winter passed, with me dazzled, drugged, dazed.

Asma stayed on the top floor of the house, in a barsati; a fair-sized terrace and two big rooms, dim, like the rest of the house, uncluttered, unlike the rest of the house. The terrace, flooded with sunshine in winter, opened on to the twisting staircase that ran along the outside and overlooked the service lane where old scooters were parked. It had the view South Delhi barsatis share, made up of great water tanks, pipes, concrete, interrupted by the filigree patterns of trees. It seemed to me the loveliest place anyone could have; secluded, part of the house yet detached from it, framed by the sky.

Sometimes I would go straight up to her when I came in to the house, having been admitted by Prem, who would give me a sly smile of complicity while I asked, Sahib hain?

No, he would say, he's gone to the market, or he's gone out with Alok-bhaiya and Sinha-sahib. Or he has a job interview, don't you remember, he was going to meet the Director of All India Radio for a job.

The interview, unfortunately, meant nothing, and a few months into the relationship I knew the market meant pills, which he might choose to pop at the end of a perfectly pleasant evening, a strip of ten white pills in dull grey foil, a guarantee of trembling hands and slurred speech.

Sinha-sahib, a second cousin of his father's, meant bhang, quality stuff, legally procured, he boasted fruitlessly, legal route to absolute distance. Ajay was nothing if not democratic about drugs. He was vastly amused when I said this, he was usually able to laugh at himself.

Meeting Sinha-sahib, though, also meant long rants about caste afterwards. Perhaps I didn't hear it earlier, I was besotted, but now I did it. After their trips to score bhang with

PILGRIMAGE

Sinha-sahib I would hear Ajay and Alok saying *Bhumihaar* and saying *us* more often.

They and Sinha-sahib nourished grievances. They despised Lalu, called him a gwaala, they saw Goswami and Chauhan as heroes, those young men who immolated themselves. Hearing them talk, I remembered the girl from the hostel marching down the road in righteous rage carrying a placard that said MY HUSBAND WILL NOT WORK AS A COBBLER.

So I would go on up to Asma's and she might have had a joint or not, she would probably be smoking a cigarette or playing JJ Cale, she would hum tunelessly along with 'Magnolia' [*the best I had*] or she'd have on 'Whiter Shade of Pale', her favourite song she said; she listened to it again and again, rewind, play, rewind, play. [*We skipped the light fandango/turned cartwheels across the floor.*] She might, on the other hand, simply be staring reflectively at the wall.

She had an enormous capacity for doing

nothing that I found restful, because she was never in a hurry about doing nothing, and she never pretended she had anywhere to go. In other words, she made leisure an art form.

She was supported by a devoted husband who made money in Dubai.

You know, Monica, he rescued me, she said. When I met him I was doing heroin and Ma was in my head, and I couldn't take her interference and her craziness. She started to want to control me, mess with me, when I grew up. It seemed to escape her that she had lost that right years ago, she added bitterly. Heroin—well, it's not something I want to do again, ever, but it insulates you, it protects you, I was able to forget who I was.

After a pause: we were all doing heroin then.

How did your Ma reconcile with that?

I don't think she wanted reconciliation. She wanted us gone; she wanted to make us disappear, like she always had.

She paused.

PILGRIMAGE

My mother hated *me*, particularly. Her sons were different—she fucked with their heads, played these crazy games with them, but in her own mad way I think she loved them, and they her. Yet Alok found Ritu, another addict, and got married on heroin, for fuck's sake, so I don't know about love, maybe I—*we*—only know about punishment. She sounded weary.

Ritu was on it too? I was unable to keep the shock from my voice, suddenly remembering Asma talking about rehab.

Oh yes, though she pretends to be so clean, won't do that much dope, will only drink expensive whisky. You should see her when the mask is off. I've held her, screaming, when she's coming off it. She goes on binges, maybe once in two years, whatever, and then Daddy comes and picks up the pieces and she recovers in expensive rehab in the States. None of our shit for her, no local rehab.

And you? Have you ever relapsed? I asked tentatively, trying to process this.

Never, she said, I'm the only one in this crazy household who hasn't and it's all because of Sameer.

But doesn't he think you possibly could, over here? I mean, I said hurriedly, seeing her face darken, with all this happening around you.

Sweetheart, the last time I did heroin was five years ago, she said with exaggerated patience.

But still, I persisted, doesn't he want you with him, wouldn't that make him feel safer?

Yeah—I guess—but I refused to go. I said he could save more if I wasn't there, and this way I could keep an eye on Ajju, too. It won't be long before he's back, though.

After a pause she said, deliberately, we might relocate. He wants to go to America, he has a brother there. He put in the sponsorship papers some time ago; right now, everything's on hold.

That was the way it was, everything was on hold she couldn't have found a better way of describing her family's situation to me.

PILGRIMAGE

I had interviews with Ritu and Alok separately and together. They were both unsurprisingly forthcoming, in the manner of junkies and alcoholics; it was as if the risks taken earned them the right to describe their journey in the most candid terms possible, with enough space allocated for their audience's genteel horror.

Ritu said she was seventeen and off her head on heroin when she married Alok. Like in the Beatles song, you know?

Man, on our wedding night we almost burned the hotel down, you know we were so freaked out by the whole ceremony thing, all that family shit, all we wanted to do was chase and the mattress caught a spark from the foil and we were passed out, didn't hear or see a thing till, fuck, there was smoke all over, remember, baby, she said, turning to Alok.

Yeah, he said, taking up the story with some relish.

They recall the waiter with the room service cart racing down the corridor shouting for help. He was shouting Madam, Madam, as if I could help him, she said.

They should have been prosecuted for starting the fire but damages were limited and they bought their way out of it, they bought their way out of trouble and drank whisky in a bar down the road with some other guests who had been evacuated.

They checked into the Taj—can you believe it, she asked incredulously—and watched the sun rise over the Gateway of India. Scared by the fire, though, they shivered and fought their way through withdrawals, they took fistfuls of pills—these were her words—fistfuls of magic little pills Daddy had got from this rehab place—and they focused just on grass and whisky.

She used those words, *focused just on*.

They were exhibited every day to friends at

soirees and ceremonies his mother organized; they got through them stoned. I had to wear Indian clothes a lot, she said gloomily, all kinds of lehengas and churidars and saris, man. It was a nightmare, you know, safety pins and under slips, that's what I remember.

You know that film crowd, they really care about clothes, everybody's always dolled up. I really hated that, you know?

I fucked off on a ship pretty soon after, said Alok, who was in the merchant navy. Just wanted to get clean, man. Couldn't take it, couldn't handle all this pressure.

Ritu went back to the States, I just cleaned up my shit, she said. I studied, and stayed clean for a while, and Alok came when he could, and then his mom became sick and we came back; he wanted to be near her.

I was surprised by this, not knowing that any of the children wanted to be in her vicinity.

Oh yeah, Ritu said, noticing my expression,

Alok was close to his mom, you must have been talking to Asma.

Yes, I said neutrally.

And now, I said, changing the subject, I mean, how long have you guys been clean?

Oh, a couple of years, Alok had a bit of a bad time recently but he's okay now, and I haven't been in rehab for a while. Boston, remember?

And the family living together, how does that affect your relationship with substances? I asked primly, consulting my notebook.

Oh Monica, Ritu said, laughing that hoarse laugh of hers, you wanna know about how we feel about Ajju?

Well, I said, surprising myself by being playful, that would be nice.

Actually, Ritu began, shooting me a sharp look.

We're fine with Ajju, Alok said seriously, cutting in, staring Ritu down. Really. Even the financial stuff. He just needs a bit of support to be on his way.

Then he added, we always looked after each other when we were younger. That's who we are.

Ritu said, Aww honey, that's so sweet.

~

We fell into a morning routine, Prem getting me my morning tea, which I dawdled over, while Ajay went to the temple, often hungover, but bathed and eager. I'd discovered, to my surprise, that he was religious, though it seemed to me a harmless sort of thing.

I thought I understood, too, why it should be so; like all believers, he needed to address himself to, abase himself before a welcoming God, he needed the reassurance, the fictive premise, of rescue. Besides, he blossomed amidst the colours and the tilaks and the red threads.

He behaved, in short, like my mother did, and I recognized that behaviour—some people needed the show, it propped them up. Asma had told me their grandmother was deeply religious—totally obsessed with ritual, man, is how she put it—and she said she was repelled by it. Hell, it was the only thing I had in common with Ma, she laughed. But Ajju was sort of into all of that, maybe because he was the younger one and spent the most time with her. He went with her to the mandir all the time, just unbelievable.

But isn't the temple-going kind of a contradiction, I'd asked her, I mean, look at him.

Asma said, Monica, the one thing you will recognize as you grow older is that people's attitudes can't be neatly categorized.

It was probably the only time she was slightly tart with me, and this stayed with me, too, because of how I began to look at him afterwards.

She interpreted him for me. Without her I would not, I think, have stayed with him as the

PILGRIMAGE

fault lines began to appear; she helped ease our relationship into a rocky permanence.

We listened to the Dead, to 'Truckin'; to the Allman Brothers Band, to 'Sweet Home Alabama', *all* the time, to Coltrane and Davis and the swirl of 'The Girl from Ipanema' [*came walking*] and I couldn't stop listening to it, so knowing and so sure, I heard it first one afternoon when we were eating sambhar and rice at Asma's. That meal I remember because otherwise food was cooked at Ritu and Alok's and Asma shared the costs. I tried to chip in with dessert and booze but they stopped me from paying for food and I remember Ritu saying, another time in their peculiarly dark dining room, that food prices had gone up and we should be careful, we should start planning meals and budgeting the week's expenses.

Alok said easily, darling I don't think we need to do that, I've got it covered.

Another time Ritu told me over a shared joint that Asma bought Ajay underwear. So touching, she said.

Ajay and I hardly went out on our own, we stayed at home with everybody else, we had music and hash, people, a motley crew besides the family, we had movies on video, food cooked by Prem, sometimes takeaway, paid for by other people, which, for some reason I couldn't understand, didn't bother Ajay at all.

We did, then, only some of the things people do at the beginning: we talked and slept and ate together and we had sex, and we always had something tight and charged when we looked at each other but the threat of the familiar began to creep up on us absurdly early, heightened by our mock domesticity, perhaps.

I began to find he was easily bored, especially sexually; he was often stirred solely by the pornographic. I began to feed him fantasies and truths to make the sex about something else, about other people, and about another self. I knew, by then, that he was often just *absent*; what kept him with me—and by this time I could not imagine being without him, without *them*—was my ability, through laughter and through sex, to show him another world, a world he had exiled himself from.

I told him about Ranjini, the time we kissed in the late evening in a classroom, the chowkidar tapping down the corridors, locking up nosily, how she backed me up against a desk, her hands in my hair. I told him of the weekends in her barsati, she came if you just put a forceful hand against the seam of her jeans. He loved the details, he asked for them, for my recollections of the noises Ranjini made when she came, for descriptions of the glazed eyes, the sounds of supplication, the begging, the pleading, don't stop, don't stop [why do we always think the other person will stop? Suddenly, maliciously, perversely?]

I gave him details, willingly, triumphantly, still amazed by my own past daring.

You're quite something, jaan, he said admiringly.

I also told him, more to amuse than to titillate, about the boyfriend who always had George Michael on in the car, he played 'I Want Your Sex' as we threaded our way through crowded streets. His Contessa had tinted glasses and steel-cold air conditioning; *sex is natural/ sex is good/not everybody does it/but everybody should*, he sang along with the chorus, bobbing slightly in his seat.

Ajay was appalled by his taste in music though he laughed and laughed at this.

He asked me, though, lying in bed, threading his fingers through my hair, sweaty after sex, if I ever wore saris and then talked dreamily about mogra flowers and red saris.

Many of the men I had known till then had deep and abiding fantasies of a woman in a sari.

If they thought they were cool the woman was riding them, sari hiked up. If they were not and had no illusions about it, the woman was getting it, in the place she should be, [and *enjoying* it, for fuck's sake] sari obligingly pushed up.

He had a *thing* about how convenient, how modestly yet explosively sexy it was, this garment, so easy to make love in, so much sexier than jeans, he said.

It was my unease about that sari that led to our first serious fight and it was about his friends, whom I had begun to loathe, perhaps unreasonably but intensely—they were dependent on him for dope, they were always around.

I thought, in the first place, he should be earning his own money and then buying dope if he must, it was bad enough that he took money from his family for this, must he support them too?

He, in turn, accused me of trying to control him and of demonizing his friends, it's the first step, he said bitterly, you think you own me.

We go back years, man, he said, we were in school together. These guys are like family.

These guys thought me uptight. I, in turn, scorned their pretence of being cool and with it—Sumit had an annoying way of singing *the future's so bright I gotta wear shades*, twirling his sunglasses. He wasn't being ironic. He'd never done a day's work and had once stolen a VCR from Alok and Ritu. Shankar had long limp hair in a ponytail, his dad was a politician, an actual neta in a khadi jacket; he'd kept Shankar out of jail on drug possession charges.

They gloated over the Masjid's destruction; over the slaughter of Muslims in Bombay, they got what they deserved, did you see what they did to that family? Sumit and Shankar even said the facts in the *India Today* story were made up. I'd heard their rants about the Bombay blasts and the punishment they would mete out to those responsible given a chance.

It was, peculiarly, in that house, and from them, that I first heard the phrase *the sentiments of Hindus*.

I did not want to discover if Ajay was of their opinion. Filled with tenderness for him, I could not forgive them for their brutishness; it seemed to me they brought out what was base in him.

I had always wriggled away, horrified, from prejudice, that much I knew, I had been on the run from it ever since I could remember.

I went to the hostel one evening soon after that fight, saying I had got a notice from the warden at the Department address and had better see what the matter was. This is what I did when I needed to get away from them, from him. There was no place to hide there, but the next day my two roommates went to their jobs and I just lay on the cot and stared at the wall. I didn't eat and I didn't smoke a joint but I listened to 'Allentown' on my small tape recorder, *So the graduations hang on the wall/But they never really helped us at all,* I listened to 'Pressure' and to 'Uptown Girl' and Billy Joel was not a name I shared with them and neither was Hall & Oates, whom I had an abiding passion for, and I went for a walk towards evening, still thinking, and the heat of the day lingered and the amaltas was in full bloom [flagrant, shockingly golden] and far far down the road gulmohar trees pushed red flowers into the sky.

I stopped at the sweet shop and they welcomed me as if I really had been away, the waiters polished a Rexene chair with a damp rag for me; they brought me jalebis and a small cup of hot tea, skin forming uneasily over it.

At night I kept the tubelight on for longer than they wanted and I wrote notes to show my guide, collating all the interviews and the narratives into coherence, keeping the tapes on low volume, unspooling with their voices and their stories, stories which had begun to feel only partially true. Perhaps, I thought, that is the nature of confession or candour, perhaps it is impossible that these or any other subjects will not fabricate, exaggerate, wilfully or unconsciously distort, shift perspectives or invent some, pretend to judge but really exonerate themselves.

Perhaps it is the nature, more to the point, of drug users, of people who've told stories about themselves to others to persuade and coerce, to get them out of a tight spot so they can go score. Everything so that they can go score.

~

When I interviewed Ajay early on he talked about the Mandrax years as his happiest. Mandrax was cheap at that time, in the early eighties, and what a high it gave you, man. He was reverential.

I waited patiently, familiar with the look on his face—all the addicts I had ever interviewed wore it when they talked about mandrax. You could get quantities of these pills from the dealers back then, the M-pill, sweet little button, you could smoke it, you could swallow it. Terms of endearment were used.

You know what we'd do, he said confidingly, we'd take a Mudrika round and round the Ring Road till the high wore off. One way, all the way down the Ring Road, get off at Dhaula Kuan and cross the road, start again. It was such a buzz.

And man, he said worshipfully, just smoking it was great. That's the best way, you know, in a pipe with grass, you have to crush the pills, mix them and then you're set, you're totally set. You just relax, you're so calm.

They called the pipe the white pipe. He

laughed. The original peace pipe, man. That's what it was.

He became somewhat cold, brisk and businesslike, shaken out of pleasurable reverie when asked if it could be swallowed, ingested. Sure, he said, you could chew it, swallow it. Its trade name was methaqualone, you know. Originally came to India as an anti-malarial.

Ajay started using heroin when he was in school. A senior, a theatre freak, provided a bunch of boys the stuff, and the annual production was the most amazing event that year. There was incredible bonding, man, he said reminiscently.

He remembered the first time, they shot it, not smoked it; they watched him prepare the spoon, burn the powder, they held their arms out for injections.

That was the last real event he remembered, that school play, and how vividly he recalled his role, he played a judge, he wore a robe and a wig and had a gavel in hand and the years from then were a blur of punishments [being taken out of college for a year and sent to various hospitals] and rewards [six months of sweet chasing till the money ran out and he felt like shit.]

He couldn't study after a BA and he couldn't get a job because he wasn't qualified to do much, so he drifted, supported by his mother's money, and he had just come out of a really good rehab scene when we met.

He hadn't done heroin for a bit, not even when his mother died because he was seeing some great chaps at the rehab place.

This was the same lot which had recommended the family as subjects, the place where I worked on and off, a dilapidated old house in a South Delhi colony, peeling paint and great goodness in the prayers before dinner and men who never slept but counselled and listened and put together food and cigarettes for all these people who had never had a job and who had lost homes and families and whose happiest memories were being off their heads, packed in with a bunch of strangers on a bus. They stole and lied and got thrown out of homes and they floated to the surface of other people's lives but those kindly men helped them pray, and stay sane, and got some of them jobs and how they all smoked cigarettes, furiously, deeply, but the nicotine was never enough, it was just a way to keep the thoughts of those sweeter pleasures at bay, a way to occupy hands that had only been good for the intricate preparation of chasing or shooting heroin.

My guide was happy with my work, I found when I went to meet him clutching piles of transcripts.

He thought the Ritu-Alok interview brilliant.

More, he thought the Ajay interview masterly.

Your rapport with the subjects comes across just in the way you phrase questions, in the way you allow them to talk.

I looked at him suspiciously. Perhaps he was having me on. Surely he must have guessed I was on somewhat intimate terms, to put it mildly, with these *subjects*.

If he had, though, he didn't let on.

This is important, Monica, he said. *Now start building the scaffolding, the theoretical framework has to be firm.*

He reeled off a list of books.

He mused about the similarity between the psychopath and the junkie.

He said, though, in parting, that I should be wary. *It seems you're spending a lot of time with these subjects, specially the sister. They can be terribly manipulative, you know.*

Ajay started slipping back into the old patterns around July, a fiercely rainy July that year, after months of mild hash-smoking and escalating drinking and pill-taking. He began to get restive and mildly abusive with me when I asked him about matters like jobs. He can't handle the intensity of a relationship maybe, said Asma worriedly.

I knew they were the old patterns because Asma told me that this behaviour would lead him to heroin, I've seen this before, she said, I know what this feels like—and I know him, Monica—and she lent me books that talked of this and I didn't tell her that I had studied it and that this knowledge was no good, it was worthless in the way knowledge felt when you haven't experienced it, when it was about other people, when it was about subjects, anonymous people or even those whose names you knew, whom you met and wrote case studies of.

I didn't tell her that I half regretted the choices that had led me to the studying of psychology, the passion for it because I wanted to understand; I wanted to understand family life [love, guilt, subversion].

I didn't tell her there was nothing, really, in my background that brought me here, investigating histories of addiction, though I had, of late, begun to count him as a serious influence, my father I mean, his odd junk heap of books, his obsession with diagnosing and curing, albeit through the administering of those peculiar potions and tinctures. [*Homeopathetic* medicine, Shireen called it.]

I didn't tell her my parents would probably hit me if they knew of the way I lived, if they had any idea of the hash and the lovers and of Ranjini. Their world could not accommodate this world they suspected I inhabited, that I had chosen to inhabit.

~

Ajay is scoring, I am sure of it. Asma thinks so, too. I have abandoned the roles of researcher, of interlocutor, even of the clear-eyed critic of his prejudices and adopted the methods of inquisitor and spy.

Everybody in the house is bored and damp patches have appeared all over the walls, the dark rooms are mouldy and the house smells of the rain which pours unceasingly from a dull grey sky. No redemption in this city in the rain, only occasional beauty in the sight of the ruins and in the trees that line the wide roads, dripping in the sulphur lights. For the rest: potholes and bad tempers, buses into which the rain comes through great gaps in the windows, a swamp-like South Campus with branches of trees uprooted lying hacked and bleeding in the muddy water.

Ajay looks like he has a lover; he looks sly and sleepy and indeed he is discovered by Asma coming back from the pusher one rainy night, he's absolutely on it. Ajay tells her to fuck off when she asks him if he's chasing. He starts to bring it home and chases boldly in the downstairs living room.

I see him on smack, on brown sugar, and despite myself I am half-fascinated, having read reams on this drug, this adulterated form of heroin [junk, skag, chaw] which contains, according to some estimates, only twenty percent heroin. The rest could be chalk, could be zinc, strychnine even. That's what the guy at the centre told me.

They heat it on foil, they catch the fumes—that's why chasing—it even looks abstractly pretty from a distance, blue clouds of smoke, the silvery glint of foil.

Heroin, I see, is the drug of the downward slide, the drug of the netherworld. It makes no claims on pleasure, or perhaps it gives the profoundest pleasure, the exquisite pleasure of the undertow. The user eschews the complex distance engendered by marijuana or bhang, the blurred delights of pills. This is serious: it is about the lack of hope and it is about death. I see him living textbook descriptions and I check the textbooks so that I can be sure. The drug causes a depression of the central nervous system, the textbooks say, the user is alternately wakeful and drowsy. The family must look for pinpoint pupils.

Now I am the family.

I see Ajay on the nod in the living room and I see everybody marshal their forces and there is brown powder in small plastic packets and in miniscule vials in the pockets of his trousers and when I threaten, melodramatically, one rainy night, to take it away, he says, perfectly coherent and clear though just a moment earlier he looked like he was about to pass out, I will kill you.

That should have been the end, but of course it wasn't. Two months of tears and threats and him sneaking off, two months of him chasing and Asma and my threatening, two months of seeing him pathetic and drugged, chasing in the loo, in the bedroom, lying on the bed where he sang 'Lay Lady Lay' to me, of course there is no sex because he has surrendered to heroin, he can't get it up and I say this brutally, hoping it will shock him but he looks at me unfocussed, sex the least important thing in this universe of numbness he inhabits; his self has gone missing and I don't know how to get at it.

In *Dare to Discipline*, the first book I ever read on drug addiction, I read a psalm, a psalm of heroin addiction, found in a phone booth, written by a twenty-year-old addict. I remember:

> *King Heroin is my shepherd, I shall always want*
> *He maketh me lie down in the gutters;*
> *He leadeth me beside the troubled waters;*
> *He destroyeth my soul.*

Its psalm-ness aside, this verse describes what I see happening to Ajay.

PILGRIMAGE

I'm smoking hash with Asma, who tells me about her mother's lover, somebody called Asad who loved her, certainly more than Amma did, he named me, she says. I used to sit on his lap and he used to sing to me.

Where did he go?

He died when I was ten. Blood cancer. Killed him in two months.

They are all matter of fact in different ways, about death and absence and people leaving. Ajay, it seems to me, is the only one who's not.

Amma left often, she told me another time. I remember her at the gate, waiting for her cab, that sardarji taxi-driver from down the road, her dark glasses on, Nana saying please stay just a while, the children miss you, she just stood still, as if she was deaf, often she left the day after she arrived.

Later they'd find out she was staying at a friend's place down the road before going back to Bombay and to life.

We sit on her terrace and the stars come out far, far away in a cloudy sky and we listen to The Who singing *Got a feeling twenty one is gonna be a good year/especially if you and me see it in together.*

She tells me more about their grandparents and about their childhood, how their grandmother chafed against her daughter's being an actress; Nani tried to be everything to us, she thought Ma had done wrong.

You're such a good listener, Monica, she says.

Asma provides a template, through her memories, of how to frame their subsequent choices, their unusual abuse, she tells me more about their father, meek but intractable. He comes from a family of landowners, we've hardly seen them, Amma couldn't stand his family and they hated her, of course. And you know, now I feel sorry for him, he left his home and family for her but the marriage was a disaster, I can see why all this caste rubbish is important to him.

She asks delicately about my family, you haven't said much, Monica, are you in touch with them? I tell her my brother Avinash drops by the hostel from time to time. I don't know why I tell her this half-truth and why I use this name we don't call him by.

I call them on Sundays from the PCO in the market where Ajay gets his pills, it has a chemist and a grocer's shop, it has a Mother Dairy booth where the token-buyers queue up with their pails and it has a chap selling flowers: pitiful gladioli and thick-petalled red roses and rajnigandha, buckets of it. I sometimes buy masses that I take for every floor of the house and the air is thick, for days, with that slightly sickening, profoundly pleasurable scent.

Sometimes I send my mother a letter, telling her I miss her cooking and I miss home. My mother writes, in turn, with real tragic flair, of their money troubles, the business is doing worse than before, your father is thinking of selling it altogether.

I think of the way my father looked after me till my brother grew to a toddler, we went on holiday to a hill station; there were snow peaks to stare at, there were rhododendrons and big silent forests with the rustle of oak and we stayed at a hotel where the children got cocoa.

I walked once with my father to visit somebody in hospital, someone who had had an operation for hernia. I felt responsible and wise, my hand in his, we walked to the colonial red brick of the district hospital and my father asked the nurse, sister, how is our boy, a friend's son; my father in loco parentis gravely managing his duties.

I felt shy, I was wearing my best dress, it had green and orange balloons on it, floating on its white. I thought hernia meant the boy's genitals had been removed, I wanted to commiserate with him but I was too small and unequal and a girl; the boy—damp-haired, large—lay in bed grimacing, asking for comics.

We spent the day there, together, dispensing water to the boy from thermos flasks. In the evening tubelights came flickering on and moths swung towards lighted windows [suicidal, importunate]. There was khichdi in a steel tiffin carrier my mother had made and rasgullas, plump and dripping.

I remember my father clowning under the lights, the boy shifting, giggling, bolster-shaped, we played cards, teen patti and rummy and my father showed us card tricks, and I remember the sudden rain when we stepped out of the building, a swift downpour that had the nurses squealing; we stood in the corridor with a stack of wheelchairs behind and watched the clean summer rain fly fine past the rafters.

They call me Mona at home. Till I was four my hair was bunched up on my head in a sort of fountain, tied with an elaborate bow. I was six when Vicky was born.

I shaved my hair in my final year in college and had my nose pierced with a beaded ring. They said they should never have let me go to college in the city, they said it was the biggest mistake they had made.

I wish I could leave him, or write my thesis, or stop smoking dope. I run to the hostel and hide, the clerks are scurrying back and forth, the smell of fried food is in the air and the smell of damp. Ritu and Alok are going to the US for a couple of months, they leave and it is September, more than half a year since I met him.

I start to write, scribbled notes:

Every drug has a nickname, a pet name, a synonym; Mandrax tablets were also called smarties, mandrakes, ludes, sopers. They were called disco biscuits in the nineteen seventies, became a party drug. Mandrax was developed as a sedative; it controlled blood pressure and was prescribed for insomnia.

Each drug, then, believed to be a revolutionary treatment for disease till it is used only for pleasure, its original use subverted, taken out of context.

Heroin is called H, Smack, Tar, Skunk, Dragon.

The whole language of drug use is specific and descriptive. Each act is encoded, provided for.

The vocabulary of the junkie consists of euphemisms. It provides for the inevitable; it forgives, in advance, the inevitable. [I slipped, he had a slip, it was a slip]

No junkie actually believes in recovery, they pay lip service to the idea and enact its codes when they have to.

I wonder if that is true.

I write dreamily:

If every piece of pleasure in your life so far has come from drugs then how can you come off them? Pleasure is, after all, the purpose of much that we do.

The drama of the junkie's life comes from a conflict with the world, which will prohibit, deny, censure him. He gains the upper hand by ceaselessly beating the world at this, by escaping, by cheating, by triumphing over a trusting world. That is how he punishes. He needs to withhold. His punishment of himself is acute, but so, too, is his punishment of others.

Most junkies are intelligent. You have to be, to beat the system so constantly and vengefully, and most of them do it with an absent grace.

Now stuff *is another irresistible word in the drug user's lexicon, so deliberately vague and so useful, so perversely against description, almost provocatively so, almost anodyne. Just:* stuff

A glossary: you have Candy and Cold Turkey, Dealer and Dexies, H, Harry, Hay, Horse, joint, junk, mainliner, smack, uppers.

A lot of this slang is American [I read it in Dobson's irreplaceable little book, Dare to Discipline, *and it stayed with me] and it's like fast food, just delicious.*

He gets off the drug. Asma calls me to be with him, she can't handle him on her own, I must be getting old, she says wryly. The withdrawals, too, are textbook: muscle and bone pain, he is cold, shivering, damp one minute, then intensely feverish, he has insomnia, restlessness, vomiting.

I hold him in my arms. His eyes burn, he says. He twitches ceaselessly. We give him the drugs that are prescribed. We watch the antidotes do their work. His nose drips. His hands begin to shake.

Perhaps I should call my father, I think somewhat hysterically, and ask him for those absurd little white pills that often, magically, work: *Camellia, Aconite, Belladona.*

He goes back to rehab, Asma gets him a place. I visit him twice a week, I am maternal, practical, and carry on with the work I had abandoned. It is simpler with him inside than roaming the world outside, he is an inmate and he is rendered impotent. He smokes, the men inside smoke their cigarettes but no dope, they say their prayers fearfully, many of them here for the third time, the fifth time, the tenth.

Diwali, in a November smoky and blue, tastes sad when I turn the corner to the rehab place because he had a slip and he scaled the walls and went and scored and he has been warned and told his friends aren't good news, I stand vindicated but it's cold comfort and Asma has been to see him but now she has gone to Dubai to visit her husband and she has said, Monica, take care of him. So here I am and I want to take care of him but I don't know how and now they are no longer around I don't know who we are, he and I, our combined reflections in the grimy mirror opposite his bed and he has a stubble, a serious one, and not very much hope in his eyes though he makes some of the old jokes and sings a snatch of Kishore Kumar to me, he says I need you, jaan, don't leave me please and he holds my hand, nervously rubbing his thumb over my palm, kissing my fingers, as if I can cure an affliction, his affliction.

My parents have not sent any threats on Diwali, only some mithai; Vicky left it at the hostel with a conciliatory note.

Maybe they are plotting.

By Christmas he's back, everybody's back and my guide is pleased with my progress and I have written the better part of a chapter while Ajay has languished in rehab and the others are away.

I do not tell my guide about my involvement with Ajay, he would say it compromises my objectivity and he would be right and I do not tell him about my hash-smoking, which is almost constant because I feel good and distant and in control and I feel obliterated yet alive and one day I find myself in a Mudrika, a Mudraker, on the Ring Road and I am stoned and there is a man rubbing up against me and I am singing in some deep part of my brain, I am singing 'Magnolia'. The ride is great and purposeful and

I find myself wanting to cross the road, get into another bus, start the journey again.

~

Our first anniversary is to entail a party, Asma says. And Ajju's turned thirty and we didn't celebrate that—can you imagine?

It's her idea, I think, but everybody is terribly excited and guest lists are drawn up every evening, we cluster upstairs at Alok and Ritu's; Ajay's not smoking dope or drinking whisky for the moment and I am resolutely staying off dope and he and I drink Campa Cola and sit cuddling on the sofa while the others drink whisky and make plans.

Satish the drug-dealer is included this time amidst arguments, you know what a sweet guy he is, says Asma passionately, we went to that farmhouse party of his, remember?

Oh yes, there was a fountain and stream inside the house. Ritu laughs.

And rocks, says Ajay laconically from the sofa.

Alok is unexpectedly stern, I don't think we should encourage him, he sold H to Ajju just recently.

Ajay pretends not to hear this.

Ritu says, Ajju shouldn't have been scoring in the first place, darling, it's not Satish's fault. That's his work.

I can't believe you said that, says Alok hotly. It's not a *profession*, you know.

Oh stop being so holier than thou, we've all been there, Satish is a great guy. Anyway, I'm planning to set up a business in his garage. You know that house he rents out down the road?

What?

Yeah, says Ritu nonchantly. It's lingerie. I've even got a name for it. Asma knows.

Everybody looks at Asma reproachfully. She hasn't mentioned this. Alok says, somewhat melodramatically, you knew?

She says, I knew, but Ritu was scared of

telling you so I didn't say anything. But really, what's the big deal?

It seems Alok doesn't like the idea of Ritu working. This is a weird ongoing battle I hadn't a clue about.

So what's it called, says Alok sullenly.

It's called Sweet Temptation, says Ritu.

I look appalled. To their credit, so do the two men. Asma looks neutral.

Back to the party, says Ritu briskly. We'll discuss this later. It's just at the ideas stage, you know.

Let's have cocktails, she says, I love cocktails, you know those pretty blue ones, what are they called?

Blue Hawaii, says Ajay.

No, Mai Tai.

Mai Tais with rum.

We need a bartender, man. He can decorate the glasses with those little umbrellas.

Cocktails, who drinks them, says Alok.

We are going to dance and dance, says Ajay, and we do, we aren't stoned, I am exultant as we dance to Hindi film songs, to the songs from *Tridev* and *Tezaab* and to rock, to sweet jazz and to Lynyrd Skynyrd, to The Band, we dance to 'Who Do You Love', we dance, once, right at the end, to Robbie Robertson, to our song.

I wear a brief black skirt Asma has given me and a purple Benetton sweater Ritu and Alok got me from the US and moccasins Ajay bought me from money he borrowed from Asma though it isn't as if he will be able to pay her back and a pair of tights Ritu loans me. They have intricate floral patterns and my legs shine desirably, I think, through them, though Ajay thinks them sluttish, like their owner, he says nastily, not even drunk.

We are getting undressed in the bedroom when he says this and I look at him in momentary clear-sighted dislike which is swamped, in a moment, by desire, as he pushes my skirt up; I peel the offending tights off so fast it's as if I never wanted to be in them at all.

Ritu is pregnant and the household is buzzing with plans. She's turning more and more to Asma for help, Asma looks opaque when Ajay says something about it. Her pregnancy puts paid to the Sweet Temptation idea, in any event, Alok has been sulking and seizes on this.

Monica, I was going to tell you, Asma says one day on her terrace, but you were so busy with your work and worried about your folks stalking you and worried about Ajju—and here she laughs, her lovely fey laugh—besides, it was so frivolous—I mean, lingerie—and here you are with those big thick books and your thesis.

I have to laugh too.

Ajay is consumed with jealousy about this new-found friendship; they have, after all, been allies against Ritu, but she says to me, Monica, we need to communicate well, when I go away who is going to take care of Ajju? I mean, you aren't always going to be around, she adds, shooting me one of her sideways glances.

She is pragmatic, I alarmed. It means she is serious about leaving.

It begins to take root in my mind, the idea that I *could* always be around, which is what, I think, Asma had tried to accomplish. I could, I could marry Ajay, what could stop me?

Ritu and Asma go shopping together in a foray into the world of diminutive garments. Ritu has endless magazine clippings on babies, on garments and feeding and teething and crawling. They start to pore over photograph albums, pulling me in, Asma points out personages and figures to us, we look at stacks of unbound photographs of her mother, posing in georgette and chiffon and Jackie O glasses.

Ajay is a curly haired baby in a pram and he's

wearing glasses at ten, beaming at the camera, here in a rickshaw, drooping, gone to score, who took that photograph, look, there's Asma, flower like, wide mouth immediately recognizable, the three of them with their mother, a rare one, Alok in dark glasses and a leather jacket, he's about to join the navy.

Here is Ajay, aged seventeen, as the judge in that school play, he looks frightfully convincing in his powdered wig and his archaic garments.

Asma, when confronted by my suspicion that she is trying to get me to marry Ajay by guile and by stealth agrees, quite calmly.

She says she thinks Ajay and I *should* marry, after all, Monica, you've rescued him already. Bit by bit, she wears down the remainder of my resistance to the idea, bit by bit it begins to seem a perfectly natural conclusion to our situation. She pays no heed to the fact that he doesn't work. It's not going to last forever; Ajju's bound to get a job.

And I'm going to talk to him, Monica, I know him. This will be good for him, this will save him. This is what he wants. I'm sure of it.

Ajay proposes to me, I love you so much jaan, you don't know, you've saved me, he says and he gives me a gold ring. Everybody is very pleased. I like the ring, it belonged to his mother, she had kept it for Ajju's wife, says Ritu.

Asma is delighted. I'm glad you are going to finally be part of the family, she tells me. Because you were, you know, right from the beginning.

There seems something preordained about the whole thing.

I don't want to, *can't* tell my parents right yet.

His father and sister come to visit, to congratulate us. They stay at the Chelmsford Club and all of us—the entire family, says Asma—have dinner with them. He is a diminutive mild-mannered man who laughs easily and of course I can't graft the father Asma has talked about on to this raconteur; he regales us with stories, even the club figures in one somewhat long-winded tale, he tells us of its history, its origins, inaugurated in 1917, apparently. Take notes, Monica, take notes, Ritu says a little bitchily, but she hugs me later, genuinely contrite, I think, at this tiny meanness.

The sister, Shawna, is, as expected, watchful, cool, briskly assessing. She has sleek expensive looking hair; she's just a little older than I am.

She named herself Shawna finally, in school, says Asma, she was named Saraswati, I think Ma had had it by the time she popped out. Nani always called her Saraswati, in any case. I keep wanting to laugh when I speak to her, remembering this dreadful tale.

She seems to think the father is her pet, she strokes his hand a lot, but he seems to like it. He is tender with all his children, though somewhat absent.

PILGRIMAGE

Asma says later it's impossible not to be fond of him, he is harmless. Even Asad was fond of him; they played chess together quite often. You just can't expect anything from him, that's all.

Nothing at all, she adds firmly.

Ajay is clean and sober and very sharp, we are both hopeful. I discover his favourite colour is brown, how did I not know this, and we play Scrabble and watch films and Asma takes us out to dinner where we eat great scoops of pork and lamb in a fiery sauce; we are, shyly, dating a bit, doing things in reverse, I start to pay, insisting on it, so we watch a movie at Chanakya and go to Nirulas next door, brushing past hanging baskets of fronds and we finish our meal off with 21 Love and hot chocolate fudge thick with nuts and we scrape the bottom of the chunky glass where the sauce has collected.

We go to the Jazz Yatra, it is clouded with hash smoke and we both succumb, we meet up with some old-timers who are standing around the poolside in ecstasy. We see a concert at Siri Fort where I think he has gone out to score [dark interval, red velvet chairs]. We go for drives, leaves in great piles on the sides of the quiet Chanakyapuri roads, the roundabouts still sleek with flowers, evenings cool, we neck in the car, parking in quiet colonies and cul de sacs like teenagers.

We thread through the summer, watching films on video, watching Sridevi in *Chaalbaaz* so many times I lose count. Ajay's in love with her in that film. We watch Hollywood films with loud throbbing soundtracks, two hours taken care of with the clunk of tape into machine, we soothe the disquiet brewing, there's no job on the horizon and the summer sun is ugly, blunting hope.

I go home for a few days, on my best behaviour, brimful of inventive lies which they seem to swallow; it seems they are happy to see me. I don't know what I feel, I only know that I welcome the heat, go shopping with my mother, sit through a puja, play cricket in the old sports ground with Vicky, consent to wearing a gold bangle tearfully got from the locker, [all gold bangles tearfully got from the locker involve long back stories] listen to a heavy-duty lecture from my father that ends with an awkward hug and a shuffling into my hand, looking significant all the while, of an envelope with cash. His partnership deal in a chemist's shop has come through, he says, there's a lot of construction going on now, you know, we're getting a shop in a mini market. The business hasn't been doing well; this has come as a godsend.

Everybody is on their best behaviour.

It won't last, obviously. I leave in a hurry, fleeing with muttered excuses about papers to present.

Meanwhile I have also started giving Ajay

money; I am getting a reasonable amount from the professor, though the work has become even more boring, which is almost axiomatic. The good thing is that I am able to do vast swathes of it mechanically, and days in the library, peering at microfilm, are routine.

Work on the thesis has almost stopped. I am inside the story I am telling. I have sacrificed my privileged position as outsider enough to collate, transcribe, ponder, measure, weigh, reason, write. I am engaged to marry Ajay, who does not work and is just out of rehab, he cannot anymore count the number of times he has been inside. He has bought me a sari, with money borrowed from Asma. It is a bandhini print, maroon with mustard. He wants me to wear flowers in my hair when I wear the sari, even though my hair is too short. He is quite firm about this and even goes out to the market looking for jasmine-sellers, the sellers of gajras you can thread around your wrist or in your hair.

PILGRIMAGE

I am hysterical by the time he comes back from hunting for flowers. I think, again, yet again, that he has gone to score.

He reassures me, manages to thread the gajra through my hair, his hands, those beautiful hands, steady, deft, tender.

Their father arrived to conduct the elaborate rituals of mourning. I hovered on the periphery, still stunned, uneasy in the presence of their relatives, unsure of my role.

Afterwards: Asma and I, marking no difference between day and night, talked about Ajay, weeping, wondering if we could have done something, *anything*. She told me the stories she already had.

Then she started to fall silent, and I realized it was over; his death had cancelled out what I had with them, it had destroyed the sureness of belonging. When I finally left though, it was to reclaim a life I could barely inhabit.

Punishment

On TV in the 1980s was the monotonous roll call of the mad and the missing, of the vacant, the tragic, the malnourished. Underneath their photographs the awful recitation: *where from, since when, to whom*.

Naresh was one of these people; he went missing for some years and when he came back, drifting into the two rooms his family lived in, he was not markedly different. He was as opaque, as amiable as he had been before he left.

He once told you of the long period when he just wandered near the train tracks, he was treated like a sanyasi by passersby even though he was young, he was given a little food, a little respect; he described how it was to stand at the edge of the tracks and feel the trains go by. That's what he did, he *felt* the trains.

PILGRIMAGE

You could *see* the rusted siding going past, the sound, furious, the smell of the tracks obliterated by that overpowering sensation of the coming train.

He was the son of your mother's uncle, her favourite uncle, who died of a heart attack when he had gone out to buy bread and eggs. This story's juxtaposition of the banal and the profound had filled you with deep unease: the uncle was wearing his night clothes, he told his wife he would be back in a moment, he collapsed on the road.

This uncle was not well off, but he was handsome and charming, virtues understood to offset his poverty. He had three children, two boys and a girl, and your mother, much older than them, undertook to help his widow bring up the children; she got the girl married [that's what it's called in this country, *to get her married*] and she helped with the paperwork so that the older boy, Puru, could inherit his father's job as a clerk.

She would give the widow a little money, and the widow would come visit her once a month, be served lunch and tea, and talk about her fate. She was a large-boned squint-eyed grey-skinned woman in a white sari and your mother was fond of declaring that she didn't know what her uncle had seen in her, he could have married anybody, she said, *anybody*.

She carried a cloth bag with a button winking in its slit.

She had a tremendous reserve of slow-burning talk.

Yet your mother seemed to enjoy the widow's company. They talked of quotidian matters with great relish, it seemed to you, and the price of vegetables was topmost on their minds. The widow often got some fresh vegetables from the mandi with her when she came to visit; you watched her pull from her cloth bag capsicums shiny and pumpkins plump, sprigs of pudina and dhania for chutney.

Naresh worked at odd jobs after he came back, he doesn't care about our family name, said Puru, he wants to lower us in the eyes of our biradari.

He worked as an office-boy and he washed utensils at a dhaba, he helped a man who made ganne ka ras, green and foamy, feeding tough stalks of sugarcane into the maw of the machine and shoving ice from a sack into grimy glasses. Eventually he started to work in a chakki down the road from the mandi.

He worked twelve-hour days and came home to sleep covered with chalky white aata which smelled warm and alive, newly sprung from grain, his eyelashes white with it, his big hands grey.

What he wanted above all, though, was to sell vegetables in that mandi near his house, a great raucous place that reeked of cow dung, fresh produce spilling on to the road, the smell of blood from the butcher's shop mingling with the smell of wet earth from the water flung over the vegetables to keep them shining.

He loved that lush, beautiful mandi, he had grown up looking down at it from the drab terrace of their two-room house, he saw the bustle and camaraderie of the sellers and looked, from above, at the shapes of ginger root and of garlic in masses, the pale green of gourds and the flashy red of tomatoes. He couldn't find a foothold there, though; the sellers were bound by kin and community. Sometimes he went and sat there, slack-jawed and happy, luxuriating in the sights. People pushed him out of the way as they jostled in front of the heaps of vegetables, bending down to prod and choose.

~

You were thirteen; curious.

PILGRIMAGE

Mona, your mother said, there's no need to keep going up to the terrace.

But there was, there was: the manservant, Pintu, spread pale, striped, wretched-looking long underwear on the ledge near his tiny servant's quarter and sometimes, pretending to be absorbed in some other task, you watched him bathing there under the tap, wriggling with glee like a boy in a village pond, wearing that underwear, dense flesh weighing it down.

You wanted to know, to feel, to investigate, that place of secrets; you saw him reach in, white foam of soap marking his body.

You declared that you would offer prayers to the sun god on the terrace every morning, standing on one leg and holding in your hand a copper pot containing water and a floating red hibiscus.

Your parents were radiant with approval.

You stood on the terrace of the new house and prayed, without conviction. You smelled

PUNISHMENT

the summer dawn before the high full heat of day, above you the clean sky, possibilities; the manservant at his ablutions, your sideways glance upon him.

There was a grah pravesh, a puja, for this new house and a little gleaming figurine, freshly painted black with red and white markings, was installed on the terrace facing outwards, staving off evil. Marigolds were thrown into the holy fire and it swallowed them obligingly, spat a little.

You longed to be outdoors, outside, away, without the volatility of fire.

That was the first time you thought, clearly, that you didn't want to be there, smoke in your eyes and the stench of ghee everywhere.

The girl in front of you at school put ghee in her hair. Her father owned a dairy. Your father said his business was doing well. He knew all the businessmen in town, he worshipped their money.

PILGRIMAGE

Your father wore, as a precautionary measure, a red gem on his finger; pundits clustered in the doorway, their satchels bursting with pamphlets and prophecies.

Your mother stood triumphant, sindoor in her hair parting, high priestess of the havan kund.

And then a velveteen sofa set from Khanna Furnishers, the best in town, was acquired, the china cabinet was crammed full and Vicky, your brother, put paper planes and boats in a garland around the ornaments and figurines congregated on the shiny mantelpiece. A mandir emerged in the small room at the front of the house and the gods were installed and polished often. Finally her gods could be safe, not kept in the kitchen in the rented houses you had lived in so far.

You smelled your mother's desire keenly, you saw how your father wanted to gratify it. He worked hard, for years he'd tried to establish this business of medical supplies [crutches, wheelchairs, oxygen cylinders grey and melancholy] now finally prospering, latecomer though he was to the world of commerce. He'd started a homeopathy clinic, his evening work, you saw his patients trickling in. He studied every night till late, it's German, he said, you have to know your patients' state of mind before making a diagnosis, you have to ask them about their dreams. He became one of the first in the town to charge what he called good money for it.

To the many pujas and the havans came the widow and her children and others from your mother's world, the world of shops selling bedsheets and big bolts of cloth, shiny and patterned, used for curtains and divan coverings, the world of the mill Naresh worked in, down the road from the mandi, next to the shops selling seeds, artificial flowers, cheap shoes and milkshakes, past the auto stand behind which the spindly minarets of the mosque rose, past the close-aired darkened shops where nighties adorned white-limbed high-bosomed mannequins and where old, old men, hunched over grimy counters, sold lace and rickrack, bukram and naaras.

Here your mother's girlhood in this small town had played out, she the just-orphaned child of refugees, brought up by relatives, it played out in the roads that led, in one direction, to the mandi and to the stout black bull who frequented the mandi, chewing his way through piles of refuse; the widow fed him lumps of gur mixed with chana every Thursday in the years Naresh was missing.

Another road led to the mandir and the lines of urchins waiting for parsad, the bell clanging as devotees stepped up to god and made themselves heard, clutching their offerings, those hapless children waiting, and on Tuesdays, the day of Hanuman, fresh hot boondi, dripping and orange, dropped into their outstretched hands.

Then, of course, were the crossroads of the bus stand, the way to the general hospital, the law courts, the prison and finally, on the outskirts of the town, to the cremation grounds.

You remember the metallic smell of the night in the old town, you ate tikkis split rough down the middle, thick with green chutney, in the lane behind the mandir in the evening and then you'd be taken through the market by Puru, collecting from this trip gas balloons, candy floss, pink with deep whorls of red, hair clips, flimsy little packets of bobby pins.

The streets would be deserted by nine except for autos racing to the bus stand, padlocks and iron grills and shutters being pulled fast on small shops, those shops selling hardware, paint, grain, daals; rats already, confidently, burrowing into sacks of grain, a few dogs curled up on piles of cement outside.

PILGRIMAGE

Near the tube lights at the corners of roads clouds of insects, uneasy.

You had to follow the rules, compulsory exercise and a balanced diet, the regular consumption of isabgol, that thick psyllium husk, and the downing of a nighttime glass of warm milk, white and accusing, without the comfort of chocolate or malt and sometimes made worse by the addition of haldi, which, in your opinion, gave the milk the appearance and taste of vomit.

The sages, you were told, swore by it.

The only exercise you really enjoyed was skipping, though they wanted you to do yoga, there was no better exercise for mind and body, they claimed.

You were passionately attached to your skipping rope, to the rapidity, the repetition, the movement, the state of dwindling to the rhythm.

Your mother confiscated your skipping rope, you're too old to skip, she said. You're a young girl now. You looked for it everywhere, with a determination that appalled her.

You found it finally and, in a rage, you told her you didn't want to exercise, your stomach hurt. You heard your mother telling your father you weren't exercising because of your period, which you had just started to get. She is shy, she said. Nonsense, your father the quasi-rationalist said, no healthy girl stops exercising just because of that. It doesn't last all month, after all. He consulted his books briskly and prescribed *Pulsitilla* and *Sepia*; these will take care of her discomfort.

You sat with her sometimes safe, though, she taught you beadwork, stringing tiny shining beads with a needle, the beads clenched together, clustered; you made an orange and blue bead purse under her tutelage. You sat with her, too, counting the just-washed clothes delivered by the dhobi, the smell of them, warm and clean, she ticked them off in her diary.

PILGRIMAGE

You read the film magazines she ordered, a man came to deliver them. In them you saw and read of film heroines and you were enthralled by the flesh you saw in those shiny photographs, you looked, and wondered at, those suggestive moles, those lips, those legs.

You now had a dance master coming to your house to teach you kathak, ghungroos half-stuck on his pudgy ankles, he was tender and paternal with your mother, he had known her since she was a girl. He had with him a little man who played the tabla, they had you practising with the neighbourhood girls, dupattas tied around your skinny waists; you were, momentarily, coy and demure, the heroines of films who would burst into bloom within a frame.

In school you danced dressed for Krishna in blue taffeta, flowers in your hair, the girls ecstatic, prayerful, genuflecting. Your parents beamed with pride seeing you on stage dancing for the gods, dancing respectably, dancing in the service of the sacred.

Your mother checked your hair for lice every Sunday with a broad, brown, blade-sharp comb, she dragged it through your hair and in the season a rain of lice fell on the white towel around your shoulders. Then the painstaking killing of the nits, fished out one by one, dazzling white, minute, cracked dead on her thumbnail.

She gave you doodh besan to put on your face, it stretched your skin as it dried, she gave you multani mitti, she did all this to make you fair and comely. She said the besan must be rubbed on your elbows and knees as well, to make them smooth and silky. She gave you sanitary towels with belts, the pads were slippery and lumpy, the belt stringy, the packet yellow. She said she had only ever used a pumice stone, but she taught you to use the sharp, fungus-smelling Anne French, underarm hair clung to the damp cotton used to cream it off; she had a round blue box of Nivea for after, slick and scented in its foil.

~

Naresh used to come over on Sunday evening to watch TV. Sunday evenings were movie evenings, the neighbourhood servants would gather and fill the dining room, where the newly bought Uptron TV had pride of place. He would sometimes arrive in the middle of the afternoon when you had just come back from school and he would be whisked around to the back of the house, given some food and sent on his way.

He had a little wisp of a moustache and a flat-nosed face. Often he would want to chat with you, he always had. He told you about the vegetables in the mandi and his dream of working there, he also told you, almost casually, about how he fell in with a company of bandwalahs. He had told nobody about those years, they had tired of asking him. That's what the widow said.

The bandwalahs, he said, were fed on time and treated well, he liked that, he was an odd-job boy for them.

But you should have told them, you said, interrupting him, suddenly passionate with dismay. You should have told your mother, she thought you were dead. She fed the bull in the mandi every Thursday.

But I came back, he said. I came back.

The hours before the groom appeared would have been the hardest. The bandwalahs, in their soiled white uniforms, dirty gold braid winking dully, collected under a tree in a park, if there was one, sitting disconsolately, fingering their instruments, on a fence, a ledge, the edge of a drain, watching the mare snort [tethered, whinnying], picking leaves off their trumpets.

The groom was always late. The mahurat was given a wide elastic margin of time, because grooms would fuss about dressing up and their mothers would weep. They sounded their trumpets, finally, confidently, when he emerged from the house, nervous as the bride but swaggering and alert, already tasting the spoils, a scooter, sometimes even a car festooned with wilting roses parked on the side.

He mounted the horse, shimmering in the dusk in its borrowed finery. They played their instruments with gusto, forcefully. Time moved again.

Naresh's sister was set on fire by her loving husband and your mother was told to discourage the widow and her children from darkening your family's ever more prosperous doorway.

You heard your mother crying when the widow's daughter died. She had arranged her wedding. The man was from a *good family*, he was a contractor. He wanted a son from her and when no son was forthcoming he poured kerosene on her and set her on fire. Your mother cried bitter tears for Pinky, the girl she had partly brought up.

You heard your father consoling your mother as she wept. You heard your mother's anxiety when she said, but what will become of them if I don't help them? You can give them money, your father replied, but don't encourage them to come here. You heard your father's fear in his reply, he was protecting his respectability, his fragile new-found kingdom.

Naresh was warned against coming to the house but scaled the boundary wall and made for the terrace, where he would be discovered in the morning. You imagined him hungry for the solidity of the terrace floor under his head, drawn to it by the lights gleaming from the house so snug.

He was missing from his own life again; often the widow would come looking for him complaining he had run away, relieved to find him safe, raging that he had caused so much trouble.

One morning you were witness to Pintu thrashing Naresh with your father's belt, at his behest, you imagined.

You remember the sound and the thin whistle of air between leather and flesh.

Each time he was hit a cloud of aata erupted into the air, as though he had absorbed it into his flesh.

There was talk of the police when he continued to make his forays into your house. Your mother pleaded, he is harmless, she said. Your father denied it. He is spying on us, he said. Your father described case studies of madmen and lunatics. He described their sexual impulses.

You could identify the examples he gave, you had read all the books in his cupboard, one at a time, he disapproved of this practice and said you would not understand; you read books on madness and you read popular science and you read studies of sexuality though he tried to censor them, you read them though you hardly recognized them for what they were, you read Masters and Johnson and those you later recognized as the borrowers and interpreters of Freud's theories. They made a rough sense to you, you threaded them together, imperfectly.

The girl is growing up, your father said. He could harm her.

Naresh had started sneaking in regardless of injunctions, beatings, threats and warnings and making his way up to the terrace like a homing pigeon.

Sometimes he shared bidis with Pintu, you could smell the sharp smell as you listened to them mutter to each other when you went upstairs.

One afternoon in the summer holidays, dazed with free time, you go up the terrace stairs while everybody is asleep, treading gently on dry leaves.

The sun beats down, relentless.

You hear laughter, smell smoke. Naresh should be more frightened, you think. He could get beaten again, this time he might well be handed over to the police, you should tell him.

Thus you proceed, but stealthily, up the stairs, and you hear a sound, not one you can identify, and you see the two men on the floor of the terrace, below the shroud of the mango tree, spread-eagled [as if in pain or from the mortification of pleasure] and you see Naresh's neck wrenched to one side as the other man finds his way.

They race to the finish while you watch, slow drip of wetness between your legs and the man moving quick in front of you, dappled sun on his sweat-streaked back. You creep down the stairs straight to the bathroom, where, crouching on the toilet seat, you have an orgasm so intense you immediately recognize it for what it is and stay where you are, sticky and blank, for minutes.

It became imperative to watch them. It wasn't easy avoiding discovery from downstairs and from upstairs; you had to creep up the stairs—luckily their preferred time was afternoon—perhaps Naresh found it easy to leave the chakki then—while your mother slept and Vicky consumed comics and Amar Chitra Kathas, slurping on an orange bar.

Pintu has served lunch and retired to his tin shed upstairs.

Tanks sit squat on the terrace, gurgling and muttering, water sloshing around their metal insides as you squeeze silently into their shadow. You watch and wait for the play to begin.

Naresh comes up the stairs, vacant and mad. Hard on his heels is the manservant, impatient and puckish. They squat, smoke, mate, Pintu always above, Naresh's head to the side, the leaves of the mango tree glossy above them, wasps gathering angry and golden near the duct of the tank where you cower. Your cotton skirt sweeps the floor.

You slip down the stairs when they finish and go straight to the bathroom where green tiles and the smell of Lux soap greet you.

This state of affairs, and this unhurried routine [theirs, yours] continued for days, maybe a month, that summer, the summer you were thirteen.

It was the dussheri season, the sweetness, the flesh of the mango was on your hands, your fingers. Torpor was upon everybody, rooms were elaborately darkened, the sun so determined its traces had to be expunged. The floor was cool underfoot and in the puja room were newly acquired brass urns filled with water and floating rose petals, the scent of sandalwood mingled with the ferocious thick fumes of dhoop-batti.

The gods slept, at ease, marble flanked.

Of course you hadn't talked to Naresh about the risk he was running.

Your mother's cactus garden was responsible for bringing this to an end. She came up the stairs one afternoon when you were squeezed behind the tanks, squatting, and the two men were under the tree. Her cacti worried her, you should have known she would come looking one day. Your father did not like cacti, he was repelled by their shape, their contours, their protuberances. He interpreted their spiny toughness as revolt and made her grow them upstairs. She'd made a little hill of cacti on the terrace and directed the manservant to look after it.

She saw you as soon as she mounted the stairs, you looked at each other directly, her gaze on both you and them. She, ashen faced, took in everything: rubbery cacti, rutting men, panting daughter, stamped-out bidis, the hose pipe lying dry and slack like a rubber snake.

Above you that day the beginning of the turning: cumulous clouds, tufted.

She left.

They, finished, getting to their feet, saw you.

Pintu knew you had been watching, the knowledge apparent when he looked at you boldly and said, merely, Didi, why are you here, do you need something? Naresh said nothing, just pulled up his trousers and turned his flat face to yours. He smiled, in welcome.

Your father complained about Naresh and Pintu to the police. Your mother was traumatized by what she had seen, she wouldn't speak to you, she wanted them locked up. They were arrested, they came to take Pintu from the house and Naresh was picked up from the two rooms that overlooked the mandi. The widow came and beat at the gate but she wasn't admitted. She shouted your mother's name at the gate, her pet name, her childhood name, but she wasn't admitted.

Your father had the height of the boundary wall increased, shards of glass and iron spikes embedded in it. Eventually they set your brother up as your protector, young and powerful he strode ahead of you into the world.

Acknowledgements

Many thanks to the following people:

My mother, Indu Singh, and my sister, Minnie Reichek; Devjani Ray, Farida Khan, Meera Sagar, Parul Bhardwaj, Sikha Ghosh.

Manju Kapur—Em—for *listening,* and for training her keen gaze on the manuscript.

Ravi Singh at Speaking Tiger, who opened up a whole way of looking at the manuscript and thus made this book possible at all; Anurag Basnet, whose extraordinarily insightful suggestions and careful re-readings contributed to it in no small measure.